WHY SHOULD I EAT WELL?

HODDER
Wayland

an imprint of Hodder Children's Books

WHY SHOULD I?

WHY SHOULD I Eat Well?
WHY SHOULD I Help?
WHY SHOULD I Listen?
WHY SHOULD I Share?

First published in Great Britain in 2001 by Hodder Wayland,
an imprint of Hodder Children's Books
© Copyright 2001 Hodder Wayland
This paperback edition published in 2001

Commissioning Editor: Alex Woolf
Editor: Liz Gogerly
Designer: Jean Wheeler
Digital Colour: Carl Gordon

British Library Cataloguing in Publication Data
Llewellyn, Claire
Why should I eat well?
1. Nutrition – Juvenile literature 2. Nutrition
Requirements – Juvenile literature
I. Title II.Eat Well
613.2

ISBN 0 7502 3645 0

Printed and bound in Italy by G. Canale & C.Sp.A., Turin

Hodder Children's Books
A division of Hodder Headline Limited
338 Euston Road, London NW1 3BH

WHY SHOULD I EAT WELL?

Written by Claire Llewellyn

Illustrated by Mike Gordon

HODDER Wayland

an imprint of Hodder Children's Books

Rachel and I love eating well.

fresh milk

chicken

We make every meal a feast.

sweet grapes

tasty lettuce

juicy tomatoes

crunchy apples

crisp radishes

crusty bread

Before I met Rachel, I didn't eat like this.

fatty burgers

fatty chips

fatty crisps

hot, cheesy pizza

I always ate the same kinds of food.

sweet cakes

sweet fizzy drinks

sweet biscuits

sweet, fatty doughnuts

sweets

sweet cake

Everyone eats food like this some of the time.

It tastes sweet ...

and it is –
well – just
around.

9

People tried to
interest me in
other kinds of food.
They tried to
make me eat well.

My Dad tried ...

The lunch lady tried ...

And so did Grandad and my mum ...

But then this new girl came
to our school ...

At lunchtime she chose the salad.

Rachel told me that eating well
means eating lots of different foods.

She said, 'Guess what will happen
if you have lots of fizzy drinks?'

'You'll be spotty and your teeth will decay.'

Then she said, 'And what do you think will happen if you never eat fresh fruit and vegetables?'

'You'll catch every cough and cold.'

And she said, 'What if you eat fatty foods all your life – what do you think will happen to you then?'

'You'll put on weight ...

you won't be fit ...

and – who knows? –
you might get sick.'

So now I eat as
well as Rachel.
Good food gives us
everything we need
to grow and
be healthy.

25

Good food helps us
to have energy
and zing ...

to have clear skin
and shiny hair.

26

It means that my meals
are more exciting now ...

I'll have the tomato salad,
the chicken curry and the
fresh pineapple, please.

And I can still have a treat now and then.

Notes for parents and teachers

Why Should I? **and the National Curriculum**

The Why Should I? series satisfies a number of requirements for the *Personal, Social and Health Education non-statutory framework at Key Stage 1.* Within the category *Developing confidence and responsibility*, these books will help young readers to recognize what they like and dislike, what is fair and unfair, and what is right and wrong; to think about themselves, learn from their experiences and recognize what they are good at. Under *Developing a healthy, safer lifestyle*, some of the titles in this series will help to teach children how to make simple choices that improve their health and well-being, to maintain personal hygiene, and to learn rules for, and ways of, keeping safe, including basic road safety. Under *Developing good relationships and respecting the differences between people*, reading these books will help children to recognize how their behaviour affects other people, to listen to other people and play and work cooperatively, and that family and friends should care for each other.

About *Why Should I Eat Well?*

Why Should I Eat Well? is intended to be an enjoyable book which discusses the importance of a healthy diet. From an early age, children make choices about the food they eat. If they know about the value of different foods, they can begin to make real choices to improve their health and well-being. Eating well is one of the ways we look after ourselves. It is important for our self-esteem.

Suggestions as you read the book with children

As you read this book with children, stop now and again to discuss the issues raised in the text. Has anyone ever tried to make them eat something they didn't want or tried to stop them eating something they did? Why was this? Do they eat school lunches or a bring a packed lunch? What kinds of foods do they choose?

Ask children to name their favourite and least favourite foods. This will show how personal their food likes and dislikes can be. Also, our tastes change as we grow older. Are there any foods that they used to dislike which they enjoy eating now?

Try not to dwell exclusively on 'healthy' foods. The message of the book is to celebrate food and enjoy its wonderful variety. Eating widely is the secret of a well-balanced diet.

Suggested follow-up activities

Ask the school cook for a copy of a weekly menu. Photocopy it for each child and ask them to think what foods Monica would have chosen before she met Rachel. What would she have chosen afterwards?

Have a 'New Tastes Day' at school. Ask everyone to bring in a food that they have never tasted. It could be a radish, a dried apricot or a small piece of cheese. Display the foods and ask everyone to try something. Can they describe the taste and texture? Do they like it?

Ask children to draw a food diary for one day, and then swap it with a friend. Do they think the other person has eaten a good mixture of different types of food. How does their diet compare to the chart on page 16?

Do a project on some kind of food e.g. pizza. What ingredients does it contain? How is it made? What are the children's favourite toppings? Ask them to draw a pizza. Visit a local pizzeria to see the different stages in making a pizza.

Play an ABC food game in which they take it in turns to memorize a list of foods and then add a new one.
'I went to the restaurant and I ate an apple.'
'I went to the restaurant and I ate an apple and some bread.'
'I went to the restaurant and I ate an apple, some bread and a piece of cheese.' etc.

Suggested cross curricular activities

Why Should I Eat Well? also gives children an opportunity to discuss things they have learned in other lessons from other parts of the national curriculum.

This book could form the basis of discussions about where food comes from. For example, you could ask children to try to find out where a particular food comes from by reading what it says on the packet. (*Geography curriculum: Knowledge and understanding of places*).

Children could also ask their grandparents or some another older person what they used to eat when they were young. Do they think that people were more or less healthy in those days? (*History curriculum: Knowledge and understanding of events, people and changes in the past: Pupils should be taught to identify differences between ways of life at different times*).

Another activity would be to show children the nutrition breakdown on the wrapping of a few different foods, and see if they can put them in order of healthiness and give reasons for their chosen order. (*Science curriculum: Life processes and living things: Pupils should be taught that taking exercise and eating the right types and amounts of food help humans to keep healthy*).

Books to read

Eek! Fly Trap by Anastasio/Cooper (Heinemann, 2000)
A picture book about a fly trap plant that has an unusual diet – including flies, sausages and burgers.

Safe and Sound: Eat Well (Heinemann, 1999)
A curriculum linked book which explains the importance of eating well.

The Very Hungry Caterpillar by Eric Carle (Puffin, 1995)
A popular picture book about a hungry caterpillar who grows into a beautiful butterfly.